50 Quick Fix Kitchen Recipes

By: Kelly Johnson

Table of Contents

- 5-Minute Avocado Toast
- One-Pan Baked Salmon
- Instant Noodle Stir-Fry
- 10-Minute Tomato Basil Soup
- Quick Guacamole
- Speedy Veggie Tacos
- 15-Minute Fried Rice
- One-Pot Pasta Primavera
- Instant Pot Chicken Tacos
- Quick Stir-Fried Shrimp
- Microwave Mug Omelet
- Easy Caprese Salad
- 5-Minute Smoothie Bowl
- One-Pan Sweet Potato Hash
- Fast Spaghetti Aglio e Olio
- Quick Quesadillas
- 10-Minute Chickpea Salad

- Rapid Veggie Sauté
- 5-Minute Pita Pizzas
- Quick BLT Sandwich
- Fast Baked Sweet Potatoes
- One-Pan Garlic Butter Shrimp
- Quick and Easy Tofu Stir-Fry
- 10-Minute Caesar Salad
- Instant Pot Mac and Cheese
- 15-Minute Garlic Parmesan Wings
- Speedy Veggie Wraps
- One-Pot Lentil Soup
- Microwave Baked Apples
- 5-Minute Hummus and Veggies
- 10-Minute Chicken Skewers
- Quick Beef Stir-Fry
- Instant Pot Vegetable Curry
- One-Pan Baked Ziti
- 5-Minute Nut Butter Banana Toast
- Speedy Avocado Chickpea Salad

- 10-Minute Spicy Tuna Salad
- Quick Chicken Fried Rice
- One-Pan Roasted Vegetables
- Quick Coconut Rice
- Instant Noodle Soup
- 5-Minute Greek Yogurt Parfait
- Fast Veggie Frittata
- 10-Minute Grilled Cheese
- Quick Spicy Peanut Noodles
- One-Pot Chili
- 5-Minute Fruit Salad
- Quick Tomato Cucumber Salad
- One-Pan Lemon Garlic Chicken
- 10-Minute Teriyaki Salmon

5-Minute Avocado Toast

Simple, creamy, and fresh

Ingredients:

- 1 ripe avocado
- 2 slices whole-grain bread
- Salt, pepper, and red pepper flakes
- Olive oil (optional)

Instructions:

1. Toast the bread until golden and crispy.
2. Mash the avocado with salt, pepper, and a drizzle of olive oil.
3. Spread the mashed avocado on the toast.
4. Sprinkle with red pepper flakes and serve immediately.

One-Pan Baked Salmon

Flaky, tender, and minimal cleanup

Ingredients:

- 2 salmon fillets
- 1 lemon, sliced
- 1 tbsp olive oil
- Salt, pepper, and fresh dill

Instructions:

1. Preheat the oven to 400°F (200°C).
2. Place salmon on a baking sheet, drizzle with olive oil, and season with salt, pepper, and dill.
3. Top with lemon slices.
4. Bake for 12-15 minutes, until salmon is cooked through and flakes easily. Serve with vegetables or rice.

www.ingramcontent.com/pod-product-compliance
Lightning Source LLC
LaVergne TN
LVHW081502060526
838201LV00056BA/2880

Instant Noodle Stir-Fry

Quick, savory, and satisfying

Ingredients:

- 1 pack instant noodles (discard seasoning)
- 1 tbsp soy sauce
- 1 tsp sesame oil
- 1/2 cup mixed veggies (carrot, bell pepper, peas)
- 1 egg (optional)

Instructions:

1. Cook noodles according to package instructions, then drain.
2. Heat sesame oil in a pan, add veggies, and stir-fry for 2-3 minutes.
3. Add noodles, soy sauce, and stir until heated through.
4. Optional: scramble an egg in the pan and mix into the noodles.

10-Minute Tomato Basil Soup

Velvety, comforting, and quick

Ingredients:

- 1 can crushed tomatoes
- 1/2 cup vegetable or chicken broth
- 1/4 cup heavy cream or coconut milk
- Fresh basil leaves, chopped
- Salt, pepper, and garlic powder

Instructions:

1. In a pot, combine tomatoes and broth and bring to a simmer.
2. Stir in the cream and season with salt, pepper, and garlic powder.
3. Simmer for 5 minutes.
4. Stir in chopped basil just before serving.

Quick Guacamole

Fresh, creamy, and tangy

Ingredients:

- 2 ripe avocados
- 1 small tomato, diced
- 1/4 red onion, finely chopped
- 1 lime, juiced
- Salt and pepper

Instructions:

1. Mash the avocados in a bowl.
2. Stir in the tomato, onion, and lime juice.
3. Season with salt and pepper to taste.
4. Serve with chips or as a topping for tacos.

Speedy Veggie Tacos

Fast, flavorful, and veggie-packed

Ingredients:

- 1 can black beans, drained and rinsed
- 1 cup corn kernels (frozen or fresh)
- 1/2 red onion, diced
- 1 avocado, sliced
- 6 small tortillas
- Salsa, sour cream, or hot sauce

Instructions:

1. Warm the tortillas in a pan or microwave.
2. In a pan, heat the black beans and corn together until warm.
3. Assemble tacos by adding the bean and corn mixture, avocado slices, and toppings.
4. Serve immediately.

15-Minute Fried Rice

Fast, flavorful, and filling

Ingredients:

- 2 cups cooked rice (preferably cold)
- 1/2 cup frozen peas and carrots
- 1 egg (optional)
- 2 tbsp soy sauce
- 1 tbsp sesame oil
- 1 green onion, chopped

Instructions:

1. Heat sesame oil in a pan or wok.
2. Add peas and carrots, and stir-fry for 2-3 minutes.
3. Push the veggies to the side and scramble the egg in the pan.
4. Add rice, soy sauce, and green onions. Stir-fry until heated through.
5. Serve hot.

One-Pot Pasta Primavera

Simple, colorful, and satisfying

Ingredients:

- 8 oz pasta (penne or spaghetti)
- 1 cup mixed vegetables (zucchini, bell peppers, cherry tomatoes)
- 2 cloves garlic, minced
- 1 tbsp olive oil
- 1/2 cup parmesan cheese
- Salt, pepper, and fresh basil

Instructions:

1. Cook pasta according to package directions, adding veggies in the last 2 minutes of cooking.
2. Drain, reserving some pasta water.
3. In the same pot, heat olive oil and sauté garlic for 1 minute.
4. Add the pasta and veggies back to the pot, toss with cheese, and season with salt, pepper, and basil.
5. Add pasta water to loosen the sauce, if needed.

Instant Pot Chicken Tacos

Hands-off, flavorful, and juicy

Ingredients:

- 2 chicken breasts
- 1 packet taco seasoning
- 1/2 cup salsa
- 1/4 cup chicken broth
- 8 small tortillas
- Toppings (cheese, sour cream, cilantro)

Instructions:

1. Add chicken breasts, taco seasoning, salsa, and chicken broth to the Instant Pot.
2. Seal the lid and set to cook on high pressure for 10 minutes.
3. Quick release the pressure and shred the chicken.
4. Serve in tortillas with your favorite toppings.

Quick Stir-Fried Shrimp

Juicy, flavorful, and quick to whip up

Ingredients:

- 1 lb shrimp, peeled and deveined
- 2 tbsp soy sauce
- 1 tbsp sesame oil
- 1 tsp garlic, minced
- 1 tsp ginger, minced
- 1 tbsp green onions, chopped

Instructions:

1. Heat sesame oil in a pan over medium-high heat.
2. Add garlic and ginger, sauté for 1 minute.
3. Add shrimp and soy sauce, stir-fry for 3-4 minutes until shrimp turn pink.
4. Garnish with green onions and serve over rice or with a side of veggies.

Microwave Mug Omelet

Egg-cellent breakfast in minutes

Ingredients:

- 2 eggs
- 2 tbsp milk
- Salt and pepper
- 1 tbsp shredded cheese (optional)
- 2 tbsp chopped veggies (e.g., spinach, tomatoes, bell peppers)

Instructions:

1. In a microwave-safe mug, whisk together eggs, milk, salt, and pepper.
2. Add cheese and veggies, stirring to combine.
3. Microwave on high for 1-2 minutes, stirring halfway through, until eggs are set.
4. Serve hot and enjoy a quick, protein-packed breakfast.

Easy Caprese Salad

Simple, fresh, and delicious

Ingredients:

- 2 large tomatoes, sliced
- 8 oz fresh mozzarella, sliced
- Fresh basil leaves
- 2 tbsp olive oil
- 1 tbsp balsamic vinegar
- Salt and pepper

Instructions:

1. Arrange tomato and mozzarella slices on a plate, alternating.
2. Tuck basil leaves between slices.
3. Drizzle with olive oil and balsamic vinegar.
4. Sprinkle with salt and pepper and serve immediately.

5-Minute Smoothie Bowl

Cool, creamy, and packed with nutrients

Ingredients:

- 1/2 cup frozen mixed berries
- 1/2 banana, sliced
- 1/2 cup Greek yogurt
- 1/4 cup almond milk
- Toppings: granola, chia seeds, coconut flakes, fresh fruit

Instructions:

1. Blend berries, banana, Greek yogurt, and almond milk until smooth.
2. Pour into a bowl and top with your choice of granola, seeds, or fresh fruit.
3. Serve immediately for a refreshing and nutritious snack.

One-Pan Sweet Potato Hash

Savory, filling, and all in one pan

Ingredients:

- 2 medium sweet potatoes, diced
- 1 red bell pepper, diced
- 1/2 onion, diced
- 2 tbsp olive oil
- Salt and pepper
- Fresh parsley, chopped (optional)

Instructions:

1. Heat olive oil in a pan over medium heat.
2. Add sweet potatoes and cook for 7-10 minutes until slightly tender.
3. Add bell pepper and onion, season with salt and pepper, and sauté for another 5 minutes.
4. Serve with fresh parsley on top, and enjoy as a breakfast or side dish.

Fast Spaghetti Aglio e Olio

Classic Italian simplicity in a flash

Ingredients:

- 8 oz spaghetti
- 4 garlic cloves, sliced
- 1/4 tsp red pepper flakes
- 2 tbsp olive oil
- Salt
- Fresh parsley, chopped

Instructions:

1. Cook spaghetti according to package directions, reserving some pasta water.
2. In a pan, heat olive oil over medium heat. Add garlic and red pepper flakes, sauté for 1-2 minutes until fragrant.
3. Toss the drained pasta in the pan with the garlic oil, adding a little pasta water to create a sauce.
4. Sprinkle with parsley, salt, and serve immediately.

Quick Quesadillas

Cheesy, crispy, and ready in minutes

Ingredients:

- 2 flour tortillas
- 1 cup shredded cheese (cheddar, mozzarella, etc.)
- 1/2 cup cooked chicken, beans, or veggies (optional)
- 1 tbsp butter

Instructions:

1. Heat a pan over medium heat.
2. Place one tortilla in the pan, sprinkle with cheese, and add optional fillings.
3. Top with the second tortilla and cook for 2-3 minutes on each side, until golden brown and crispy.
4. Slice and serve with salsa, sour cream, or guacamole.

10-Minute Chickpea Salad

Light, protein-packed, and quick

Ingredients:

- 1 can chickpeas, drained and rinsed
- 1 cucumber, diced
- 1/2 red onion, finely chopped
- 1 tbsp olive oil
- 1 tbsp lemon juice
- Salt and pepper
- Fresh parsley, chopped (optional)

Instructions:

1. Combine chickpeas, cucumber, and onion in a bowl.
2. Drizzle with olive oil and lemon juice, season with salt and pepper.
3. Toss to combine and garnish with parsley. Serve immediately.

Rapid Veggie Sauté

Colorful, healthy, and ready in minutes

Ingredients:

- 1 cup broccoli florets
- 1 red bell pepper, sliced
- 1 zucchini, sliced
- 2 tbsp olive oil
- 1 tsp garlic, minced
- Salt and pepper

Instructions:

1. Heat olive oil in a pan over medium heat.
2. Add garlic and sauté for 30 seconds.
3. Add vegetables and stir-fry for 4-5 minutes until tender but still crisp.
4. Season with salt and pepper and serve as a side dish or over rice.

5-Minute Pita Pizzas

Quick, cheesy, and customizable

Ingredients:

- 2 pita bread rounds
- 1/4 cup pizza sauce
- 1 cup shredded mozzarella cheese
- 1/2 cup pepperoni slices or veggies (optional)
- Dried oregano, basil, or Italian seasoning

Instructions:

1. Preheat the oven to 400°F (200°C).
2. Spread pizza sauce on each pita bread.
3. Sprinkle with cheese and add desired toppings.
4. Bake for 5-7 minutes, until the cheese is melted and bubbly.
5. Sprinkle with seasonings and serve hot.

Quick BLT Sandwich

Classic, crispy, and satisfying

Ingredients:

- 2 slices of whole-grain or white bread
- 4 slices of cooked bacon
- 2-3 leaves of lettuce
- 2 tomato slices
- Mayonnaise

Instructions:

1. Toast the bread until golden brown.
2. Spread mayonnaise on both slices of toast.
3. Layer with bacon, lettuce, and tomato slices.
4. Close the sandwich and serve immediately.

Fast Baked Sweet Potatoes

Tender, nutritious, and easy to make

Ingredients:

- 2 medium sweet potatoes
- Olive oil
- Salt and pepper

Instructions:

1. Preheat the oven to 400°F (200°C).
2. Prick sweet potatoes with a fork and rub with olive oil, salt, and pepper.
3. Place on a baking sheet and bake for 35-40 minutes, until soft and tender.
4. Slice open and serve with toppings like butter, cinnamon, or sour cream.

One-Pan Garlic Butter Shrimp

Garlicky, buttery, and juicy

Ingredients:

- 1 lb shrimp, peeled and deveined
- 2 tbsp butter
- 3 cloves garlic, minced
- 1 tbsp lemon juice
- Salt and pepper
- Fresh parsley, chopped

Instructions:

1. Heat butter in a pan over medium heat.
2. Add garlic and sauté for 1 minute.
3. Add shrimp and cook for 2-3 minutes per side until pink and cooked through.
4. Drizzle with lemon juice, season with salt and pepper, and sprinkle with parsley. Serve immediately.

Quick and Easy Tofu Stir-Fry

Simple, savory, and plant-based

Ingredients:

- 1 block firm tofu, drained and cubed
- 2 tbsp soy sauce
- 1 tbsp sesame oil
- 1/2 cup mixed veggies (bell peppers, broccoli, carrots)
- 1 tbsp hoisin sauce (optional)

Instructions:

1. Heat sesame oil in a pan over medium heat.
2. Add tofu cubes and cook for 4-5 minutes, turning until golden and crispy.
3. Add mixed veggies and stir-fry for 3-4 minutes until tender.
4. Drizzle with soy sauce and hoisin sauce, and toss to coat. Serve hot.

10-Minute Caesar Salad

Crisp, creamy, and full of flavor

Ingredients:

- 4 cups romaine lettuce, chopped
- 1/4 cup Caesar dressing
- 1/4 cup grated parmesan cheese
- Croutons

Instructions:

1. Toss chopped lettuce with Caesar dressing in a large bowl.
2. Sprinkle with parmesan cheese and add croutons.
3. Serve immediately as a side or light meal.

Instant Pot Mac and Cheese

Creamy, cheesy, and made in a flash

Ingredients:

- 8 oz elbow macaroni
- 2 cups water
- 1 cup milk
- 2 cups shredded cheddar cheese
- 1 tbsp butter
- Salt and pepper

Instructions:

1. Add macaroni, water, and a pinch of salt to the Instant Pot.
2. Seal the lid and cook on high pressure for 4 minutes.
3. Quick release the pressure and stir in milk, cheese, and butter.
4. Season with salt and pepper and serve immediately.

15-Minute Garlic Parmesan Wings

Crispy, savory, and irresistible

Ingredients:

- 12 chicken wings
- 2 tbsp olive oil
- 1/4 cup grated parmesan cheese
- 3 cloves garlic, minced
- Salt and pepper
- Fresh parsley, chopped

Instructions:

1. Preheat the oven to 425°F (220°C).
2. Toss chicken wings in olive oil, garlic, salt, and pepper.
3. Bake for 12-15 minutes until crispy and golden.
4. Toss wings in parmesan cheese and garnish with parsley. Serve hot.

Speedy Veggie Wraps

Fresh, crunchy, and packed with nutrients

Ingredients:

- 2 whole-wheat wraps or tortillas
- 1/2 cup hummus
- 1 cup mixed veggies (cucumber, bell pepper, spinach, avocado)
- Salt and pepper

Instructions:

1. Spread hummus on each tortilla.
2. Layer with fresh veggies and season with salt and pepper.
3. Roll up the wraps tightly and slice into halves. Serve immediately.

One-Pot Lentil Soup

Hearty, comforting, and all in one pot

Ingredients:

- 1 cup dried lentils, rinsed
- 1 can diced tomatoes
- 4 cups vegetable broth
- 1 onion, chopped
- 2 carrots, diced
- 2 cloves garlic, minced
- 1 tsp cumin
- Salt and pepper
- Fresh parsley, chopped (optional)

Instructions:

1. In a large pot, combine lentils, tomatoes, vegetable broth, onion, carrots, and garlic.
2. Season with cumin, salt, and pepper.
3. Bring to a boil, then reduce heat and simmer for 25-30 minutes, until lentils are tender.
4. Garnish with fresh parsley and serve hot.

Microwave Baked Apples

Warm, sweet, and easy to make

Ingredients:

- 2 apples, cored
- 1 tbsp cinnamon
- 1 tbsp honey or maple syrup
- 1 tbsp butter (optional)

Instructions:

1. Place apples in a microwave-safe bowl and fill the centers with cinnamon, honey, and butter.
2. Cover the bowl with a microwave-safe lid or plate.
3. Microwave on high for 3-5 minutes, until the apples are tender.
4. Serve warm as a simple dessert or snack.

5-Minute Hummus and Veggies

Quick, healthy, and refreshing

Ingredients:

- 1/2 cup hummus
- 1 cucumber, sliced
- 1 bell pepper, sliced
- 1/2 cup cherry tomatoes
- Fresh parsley (optional)

Instructions:

1. Arrange sliced veggies on a plate.
2. Serve with hummus on the side for dipping.
3. Garnish with fresh parsley, if desired, and enjoy as a snack or appetizer.

10-Minute Chicken Skewers

Tender, flavorful, and grilled to perfection

Ingredients:

- 2 chicken breasts, cut into cubes
- 2 tbsp olive oil
- 1 tbsp lemon juice
- 1 tsp paprika
- Salt and pepper
- Wooden skewers (soaked in water)

Instructions:

1. Preheat grill or grill pan to medium-high heat.
2. In a bowl, combine olive oil, lemon juice, paprika, salt, and pepper.
3. Thread chicken cubes onto skewers and brush with marinade.
4. Grill for 5-7 minutes on each side, until chicken is cooked through.
5. Serve hot with your favorite dipping sauce.

Quick Beef Stir-Fry

Savory, quick, and full of flavor

Ingredients:

- 1 lb beef sirloin, thinly sliced
- 1 tbsp soy sauce
- 1 tbsp sesame oil
- 1 bell pepper, sliced
- 1/2 onion, sliced
- 1 tbsp ginger, minced
- 1 clove garlic, minced

Instructions:

1. Heat sesame oil in a pan over medium-high heat.
2. Add beef and stir-fry for 3-4 minutes until browned.
3. Add bell pepper, onion, ginger, and garlic, and stir-fry for another 2-3 minutes.
4. Add soy sauce and toss everything together. Serve immediately.

Instant Pot Vegetable Curry

Rich, aromatic, and quick to prepare

Ingredients:

- 2 cups mixed vegetables (carrots, peas, potatoes, etc.)
- 1 can coconut milk
- 1 cup vegetable broth
- 2 tbsp curry powder
- 1 onion, chopped
- 2 cloves garlic, minced
- Salt and pepper

Instructions:

1. Set the Instant Pot to sauté mode.
2. Add onion and garlic, sautéing for 2-3 minutes until softened.
3. Add mixed vegetables, coconut milk, vegetable broth, curry powder, salt, and pepper.
4. Seal the lid and cook on high pressure for 5 minutes.
5. Quick release the pressure, stir, and serve with rice or naan.

One-Pan Baked Ziti

Comforting, cheesy, and all baked together

Ingredients:

- 12 oz ziti pasta
- 1 jar marinara sauce
- 2 cups shredded mozzarella cheese
- 1/2 cup grated parmesan cheese
- 1/2 cup ricotta cheese
- Fresh basil, chopped (optional)

Instructions:

1. Preheat oven to 375°F (190°C).
2. Cook pasta according to package directions, then drain.
3. In a baking dish, combine cooked pasta and marinara sauce.
4. Layer with mozzarella, ricotta, and parmesan cheeses.
5. Bake for 15-20 minutes, until cheese is melted and bubbly.
6. Garnish with fresh basil and serve hot.

5-Minute Nut Butter Banana Toast

Quick, healthy, and satisfying

Ingredients:

- 2 slices whole-grain bread
- 2 tbsp almond or peanut butter
- 1 banana, sliced
- Honey (optional)

Instructions:

1. Toast the bread until golden brown.
2. Spread nut butter on each slice.
3. Top with banana slices and drizzle with honey, if desired.
4. Serve immediately for a quick, energizing snack.

Speedy Avocado Chickpea Salad

Creamy, crunchy, and packed with nutrients

Ingredients:

- 1 ripe avocado, mashed
- 1 can chickpeas, drained and rinsed
- 1/2 red onion, chopped
- 1 tbsp olive oil
- 1 tbsp lemon juice
- Salt and pepper

Instructions:

1. In a bowl, mash the avocado.
2. Add chickpeas, onion, olive oil, and lemon juice.
3. Season with salt and pepper, then toss everything together.
4. Serve immediately as a salad or sandwich filling.

10-Minute Spicy Tuna Salad

Fresh, zesty, and packed with protein

Ingredients:

- 1 can tuna, drained
- 2 tbsp mayonnaise
- 1 tbsp sriracha sauce (adjust to taste)
- 1 tbsp soy sauce
- 1 green onion, chopped
- 1/2 cucumber, diced
- Salt and pepper

Instructions:

1. In a bowl, mix together tuna, mayonnaise, sriracha sauce, soy sauce, and green onion.
2. Add diced cucumber and season with salt and pepper.
3. Serve on its own, in a sandwich, or with crackers.

Quick Chicken Fried Rice

Savory, satisfying, and full of flavor

Ingredients:

- 1 cup cooked rice (preferably cold)

- 1/2 cup cooked chicken, diced
- 1/2 cup frozen peas and carrots
- 2 eggs, scrambled
- 2 tbsp soy sauce
- 1 tbsp sesame oil
- 1 green onion, chopped

Instructions:

1. Heat sesame oil in a pan over medium heat.
2. Add peas and carrots and cook for 2-3 minutes.
3. Push veggies to the side and scramble eggs in the same pan.
4. Add rice, chicken, soy sauce, and green onion. Stir to combine and cook for 3-5 minutes until heated through. Serve hot.

One-Pan Roasted Vegetables

Simple, healthy, and delicious

Ingredients:

- 2 cups mixed vegetables (carrots, bell peppers, zucchini, etc.)
- 2 tbsp olive oil
- 1 tsp dried rosemary

- Salt and pepper

Instructions:

1. Preheat oven to 425°F (220°C).

2. Toss vegetables with olive oil, rosemary, salt, and pepper.

3. Spread on a baking sheet in a single layer.

4. Roast for 15-20 minutes, stirring halfway through, until vegetables are tender and golden. Serve immediately.

Quick Coconut Rice

Fragrant, creamy, and perfectly paired with any dish

Ingredients:

- 1 cup jasmine rice
- 1 can coconut milk
- 1/2 cup water
- 1/2 tsp salt

Instructions:

1. Rinse rice under cold water until the water runs clear.

2. In a saucepan, combine rice, coconut milk, water, and salt.

3. Bring to a boil, then reduce heat to low and cover.

4. Simmer for 15-18 minutes, until rice is tender and the liquid is absorbed. Fluff with a fork and serve.

Instant Noodle Soup

Quick, comforting, and customizable

Ingredients:

- 1 package instant noodles
- 2 cups water
- 1 tbsp soy sauce
- 1/2 tsp sesame oil
- 1 green onion, chopped
- 1 boiled egg (optional)

Instructions:

1. Boil water in a pot and add the instant noodles.
2. Cook noodles according to package directions (usually 3-5 minutes).
3. Add soy sauce, sesame oil, and green onions to the pot.
4. Top with a boiled egg if desired and serve hot.

5-Minute Greek Yogurt Parfait

Creamy, fruity, and healthy

Ingredients:

- 1 cup Greek yogurt
- 1/4 cup granola
- 1/2 cup mixed berries (strawberries, blueberries, raspberries)
- Honey (optional)

Instructions:

1. In a glass or bowl, layer Greek yogurt, granola, and berries.
2. Drizzle with honey if desired.
3. Serve immediately as a snack or breakfast.

Fast Veggie Frittata

Light, savory, and perfect for any meal

Ingredients:

- 4 eggs
- 1/2 cup bell pepper, diced
- 1/2 cup spinach, chopped
- 1/4 cup cheese (cheddar, feta, etc.)
- Salt and pepper

Instructions:

1. Preheat oven to 375°F (190°C).
2. In a skillet, sauté bell pepper and spinach until softened.
3. In a bowl, whisk eggs, cheese, salt, and pepper.
4. Pour eggs over veggies in the skillet and cook on low heat for 2-3 minutes.
5. Transfer to the oven and bake for 5-7 minutes, until eggs are set. Serve hot.

10-Minute Grilled Cheese

Golden, melty, and always a favorite

Ingredients:

- 2 slices bread
- 2 slices cheese (cheddar, American, etc.)
- 1 tbsp butter

Instructions:

1. Heat a pan over medium heat.
2. Butter one side of each slice of bread.
3. Place cheese between the slices, with buttered sides facing out.
4. Grill for 2-3 minutes per side until golden brown and cheese is melted. Serve immediately.

Quick Spicy Peanut Noodles

Rich, spicy, and full of flavor

Ingredients:

- 8 oz noodles (spaghetti or rice noodles)
- 2 tbsp peanut butter
- 1 tbsp soy sauce
- 1 tbsp sriracha sauce (adjust to taste)
- 1 tbsp sesame oil
- 1 tsp honey
- 1 green onion, chopped

Instructions:

1. Cook noodles according to package directions and drain.
2. In a bowl, whisk together peanut butter, soy sauce, sriracha, sesame oil, and honey.
3. Toss noodles with peanut sauce and top with green onions. Serve immediately.

One-Pot Chili

Hearty, savory, and full of bold flavors

Ingredients:

- 1 lb ground beef (or turkey)
- 1 onion, chopped
- 2 cloves garlic, minced
- 1 can (15 oz) kidney beans, drained and rinsed
- 1 can (15 oz) black beans, drained and rinsed
- 1 can (15 oz) diced tomatoes
- 1 can (6 oz) tomato paste
- 1 tbsp chili powder
- 1 tsp cumin
- Salt and pepper to taste

Instructions:

1. In a large pot, brown the ground beef with chopped onion and garlic over medium heat.
2. Add beans, diced tomatoes, tomato paste, chili powder, cumin, salt, and pepper.
3. Stir to combine and simmer for 15-20 minutes, letting the flavors meld together.
4. Serve hot, topped with sour cream, cheese, or cilantro if desired.

5-Minute Fruit Salad

Refreshing, sweet, and perfect for a quick snack

Ingredients:

- 1 cup strawberries, sliced
- 1 cup grapes, halved
- 1 orange, peeled and segmented
- 1 banana, sliced
- 1/2 cup blueberries
- 1 tbsp honey (optional)

Instructions:

1. Combine all the fruit in a bowl.
2. Drizzle with honey if desired, and toss gently to combine.
3. Serve immediately and enjoy!

Quick Tomato Cucumber Salad

Light, crisp, and zesty

Ingredients:

- 1 cucumber, sliced
- 2 tomatoes, diced
- 1/4 red onion, thinly sliced
- 2 tbsp olive oil
- 1 tbsp red wine vinegar
- Salt and pepper to taste
- Fresh parsley for garnish (optional)

Instructions:

1. In a bowl, combine cucumber, tomatoes, and red onion.
2. Drizzle with olive oil and vinegar, then season with salt and pepper.
3. Toss to combine and garnish with fresh parsley if desired. Serve immediately.

One-Pan Lemon Garlic Chicken

Juicy, flavorful, and so easy to make

Ingredients:

- 4 boneless, skinless chicken breasts
- 3 cloves garlic, minced
- 2 tbsp olive oil
- 1 lemon, zest and juice
- Salt and pepper to taste
- Fresh parsley for garnish

Instructions:

1. Preheat oven to 400°F (200°C).
2. In a small bowl, mix together garlic, olive oil, lemon zest and juice, salt, and pepper.
3. Place chicken breasts on a baking sheet and brush with the lemon garlic mixture.
4. Bake for 20-25 minutes or until chicken is fully cooked.
5. Garnish with fresh parsley and serve hot.

10-Minute Teriyaki Salmon

Sweet, savory, and perfect for a quick dinner

Ingredients:

- 2 salmon fillets
- 2 tbsp teriyaki sauce
- 1 tbsp sesame oil
- 1 tsp grated ginger
- 1 tbsp sesame seeds (optional)
- Green onions, chopped for garnish (optional)

Instructions:

1. Heat sesame oil in a skillet over medium heat.
2. Add salmon fillets and cook for 3-4 minutes on each side until golden and cooked through.
3. Drizzle with teriyaki sauce and grated ginger during the last minute of cooking.
4. Sprinkle with sesame seeds and green onions before serving.

www.ingramcontent.com/pod-product-compliance
Lightning Source LLC
LaVergne TN
LVHW081501060526
838201LV00056BA/2879